797,885 Books

are available to read at

www.ForgottenBooks.com

Forgotten Books' App
Available for mobile, tablet & eReader

ISBN 978-1-330-63889-7
PIBN 10085924

This book is a reproduction of an important historical work. Forgotten Books uses
state-of-the-art technology to digitally reconstruct the work, preserving the original format
whilst repairing imperfections present in the aged copy. In rare cases, an imperfection in
the original, such as a blemish or missing page, may be replicated in our edition. We do,
however, repair the vast majority of imperfections successfully; any imperfections that
remain are intentionally left to preserve the state of such historical works.

Forgotten Books is a registered trademark of FB &c Ltd.
Copyright © 2017 FB &c Ltd.
FB &c Ltd, Dalton House, 60 Windsor Avenue, London, SW19 2RR.
Company number 08720141. Registered in England and Wales.

For support please visit www.forgottenbooks.com

1 MONTH OF
FREE
READING

at

www.ForgottenBooks.com

By purchasing this book you are eligible for one month membership to ForgottenBooks.com, giving you unlimited access to our entire collection of over 700,000 titles via our web site and mobile apps.

To claim your free month visit: www.forgottenbooks.com/free85924

* Offer is valid for 45 days from date of purchase. Terms and conditions apply.

English
Français
Deutsche
Italiano
Español
Português

www.forgottenbooks.com

Mythology Photography **Fiction**
Fishing Christianity **Art** Cooking
Essays Buddhism Freemasonry
Medicine **Biology** Music **Ancient
Egypt** Evolution Carpentry Physics
Dance Geology **Mathematics** Fitness
Shakespeare **Folklore** Yoga Marketing
Confidence Immortality Biographies
Poetry **Psychology** Witchcraft
Electronics Chemistry History **Law**
Accounting **Philosophy** Anthropology
Alchemy Drama Quantum Mechanics
Atheism Sexual Health **Ancient History**
Entrepreneurship Languages Sport
Paleontology Needlework Islam
Metaphysics Investment Archaeology
Parenting Statistics Criminology
Motivational

HOUSING . .
. . BY . .
VOLUNTARY
ENTERPRISE

BEING CHIEFLY

*AN EXAMINATION OF THE ARGU-
MENTS CONCERNING THE PRO-
VISION OF DWELLING-HOUSES BY
MUNICIPAL AUTHORITIES UNDER
PART III. OF THE HOUSING OF
THE WORKING CLASSES ACTS . .*

BY

JAMES PARSONS

BARRISTER-AT-LAW

𝔏𝔬𝔫𝔡𝔬𝔫

P. S. KING & SON

ORCHARD HOUSE, WESTMINSTER

1903

HD 7333
.A3P3

REESE

BRADBURY, AGNEW, & CO. LD., PRINTERS,
LONDON AND TONBRIDGE.

TO MY FRIEND

THOMAS MACKAY

TO WHOM I AM INDEBTED FOR SUGGESTIONS,

ENCOURAGEMENT, AND AID

𝕴 𝕯𝖊𝖉𝖎𝖈𝖆𝖙𝖊

THIS LITTLE BOOK.

UNITED UNIVERSITY CLUB,
PALL MALL EAST,
February, 1903

157705

CONTENTS.

———◆———

CHAP.   PAGE

I. PRELIMINARY 1

II. ACHIEVEMENTS OF VOLUNTARY ENTER-
PRISE 9

III. CONDITIONS OF EFFICIENCY . . . 21

IV. STORY OF A BUILDING COMPANY . . 36

V. INEFFICIENCY OF MUNICIPAL BUILDING . 57

VI. PUBLIC DANGERS OF MUNICIPAL BUILDING 68

VII. SANITARY DEFECTS AND MUNICIPAL
BUILDING 77

VIII. SANITARY DEFECTS AND AN IMPROVED
ART OF LIVING 95

IX. GROWTH OF PUBLIC BURDENS . . 101

X. CONCLUSION 108

———————————

APPENDIX.

CENSUS OF ENGLAND AND WALES, 1901, COUNTY
OF LONDON, TABLE XIX. 115

HOUSING

BY

VOLUNTARY ENTERPRISE.

===========

CHAPTER I.

PRELIMINARY.

THIS little volume is concerned with the
provision of dwellings for the poorer part
of the population under one only of many
aspects. Amid the chorus of suggestions
which have been made towards improvement
in the homes of the people one cry seems
now to overpower all other voices. There
is a widespread demand that the State should
assume increased responsibility for the provision of houses for wage-earners, and in
discharge of this responsibility should undertake the building and ownership of dwellings.

PRELIMINARY.

The State has hitherto secured the provision of dwellings only when it has displaced occupiers of the labouring class in the course of effecting a public improvement. This policy, it may be observed, has led to a heavy loss of public money, and is of doubtful utility. The payment of high prices for insanitary property and the fall in value of sites restricted to residential purposes have involved the ratepayers of London in losses which since 1876 amount to £2,354,000, as appears by the latest Return to the London County Council, to March 31st, 1902 (Summary of Return I. p. 5).

This policy has led, moreover, to the erection of dwellings on sites which would be more beneficially used for general commercial purposes. It has tended, furthermore, to hinder the dispersal of industries by making it easier for wage-earners to reside in the central districts. The wage-earning classes have not received benefits equivalent to these sacrifices. No such sacrifices were necessary, inasmuch as voluntary enterprise might have been safely trusted to supply reasonable requirements in the matter of house-room. Its achievements in the last ten years, as set forth in the following pages, abundantly attest its vitality. Public responsibility, then, has hitherto been restricted within limits defined by the displacement of population for public purposes. It is not proposed to discuss this first extension of the responsibility of the State.

A considerable section of those who mould public opinion has declared itself in favour of still further extending the responsibility of the State so as to include the provision of houses for wage-earners apart from any displacement by public authority. It is urged that the work of housing the people should be undertaken on a large scale by the county councils and the borough councils, and these bodies are invited to use the powers which have been conferred upon them by the Legislature[1] of acquiring sites and building houses by means of borrowed money charged with interest upon the rates.

In pursuance of this policy the London County Council has undertaken schemes for

[1] Housing of the Working Classes Acts, 1890 and 1900, Part III.; London Government Act, 1899.

the ultimate accommodation of 67,000 persons on 348 acres at a cost of £230,000 for the sites, and £2,961,000 for the buildings, as appears in the latest Returns to the Council (Return III. p. 9).

It is this novel extension of public responsibility which it is proposed to examine.

A further word of explanation is desirable. A marked feature of the present time is the growing consciousness of personal responsibility for the consequences of acts which affect the welfare of others. The sanitary laws are based on a public recognition of this responsibility in matters which touch the public health. Some such laws seem to be a necessity in a community in which the care of the public health has become recognised as a public responsibility, in which the conditions of healthy living are widely misunderstood, and in which the thickness of population makes insanitary ways especially harmful. It is, however, no part of the present purpose to discuss the expediency of the existing regulations of the Public Health Acts and the Building Acts. It is clear, furthermore, that the consciousness of responsibility which has realized itself in these laws goes beyond the scope of law; it is personal, incumbent on the individual, compelling him, in proportion as it is felt, to ameliorate the sanitary conditions of those who live within the range of his influence. The existence of this consciousness of responsibility is a fact. It is not proposed to examine its range or to become entangled in any discussion as to the roots, in reason and in morals, from which it springs. The object of this volume is to estimate the probable result of the new proposals as a method of giving effect to it.

Are wage-earners likely through the action of the councils to get better houses and more of them ?

Furthermore, it is not desired to challenge the democratic basis of local government. The councils, however, like other human institutions, have their limits of usefulness. Experience, discussion, and the judgment of reasonable men are needed in order to ascertain the bounds of their beneficial activity. This volume is written as a contribution towards such a discussion. It is desired to raise the question whether the provision of houses for wage-earners, as is now proposed, is a function which it is well, in the public interest, to entrust to municipal authorities.

The author's experience in the work of housing wage-earners has been restricted to London. The facts, therefore, which are mentioned in enforcement of the arguments advanced are drawn from London. The principles, however, which the facts illustrate, cover wider ground, and are applicable wherever the housing of the people is found or is alleged to be below a reasonable standard of requirement.

Municipal enterprise in house-building is advocated on various grounds.

1. The intervention of the State is mainly invoked on the plea of necessity. It is said that voluntary enterprise has failed in the task of providing house-room, and that houses will not be built unless the State intervene for the purpose of building them. The validity of this allegation is examined in Chapter II.

2. The advocacy of State intervention in house-building is an instance of a

growing tendency. Whenever anything is felt to be amiss, men invoke the action of the State in a spirit of faith and without much questioning. They do not pause to consider whether the matter be one in which improvement can reasonably be expected through the agency of public bodies. It is proposed, therefore, to examine the conditions which promote efficiency in the work of providing houses suitable to the requirements of wage-earners, and in the light of such an examination to estimate the influence which municipal action is likely to exercise on the housing of the people. These matters are considered in Chapters III. and V.

By way of illustrating the conditions of efficiency, an account is given in Chapter IV. of the work of the East End Dwellings Company, Limited, a commercial undertaking founded in 1884, with the management of which the author has been connected from the beginning.

3. The claim that the State should embark on house-building is often urged by pointing an indignant finger at sanitary defects. This is a cheap and effective argument in popular

discussion. These defects, therefore, are analysed in Chapter VII. with a view to appraise the remedial value of the proposed intervention of the State.

It is plain, furthermore, that the appearance of the State as a purveyor and owner of houses, is attended by positive dangers and drawbacks. These are set forth in Chapter VI. The reader is, in conclusion, invited to strike the balance between these disadvantages and the allurements of the advocates of the new policy as they appear in the light of the examination of them contained in the earlier chapters.

CHAPTER II.

ACHIEVEMENTS OF VOLUNTARY ENTERPRISE.

IT is alleged by some advocates of municipal house-building that voluntary enterprise has failed in the task of providing house-room, and that houses will not be built unless the State intervene for the purpose of building them. This is a plain issue, on which opportune and cogent evidence is available.

Even before the publication of the Census returns of 1901 there seemed good reason to dissent from the proposal that the State should intervene in order to provide houses for wage-earners. It seemed to many of those who had experience of the actual work of building and owning dwellings that the advocates of State intervention were deficient in knowledge and hasty in inference. Confusion of mind was prevalent between the alleged duty of the State to provide homes for the people and its duty to supervise dwellings in the interest of the public health. The presence of sanitary evils, due to defects in character and in civilization, which fell within the provisions of existing legislation, was urged as a plea for imposing on the State new responsibilities. More important still, the achievements of free enterprise were forgotten or ignored. While men were debating, wrangling and crying aloud to the State, there were silently rising from the ground houses innumerable, the offspring of commercial impulse, equivalent to an immense city. It seemed evident to those who were conversant with the facts that great caution should be used before committing the State to the new policy.

The need of caution is abundantly confirmed by the results of the recent Census. The facts established by the Census, and the inferences fairly deducible from them, are in strong confirmation of the opinion of those who regard the proposed intervention of the State as both unnecessary and undesirable.

On two points the Census returns speak clearly.

Voluntary enterprise, in the first place, has shown during the decade abundant vitality in providing the houses required for the large increase in the population of Greater London, and for a considerable transference of population within the County of London.

This result, in the second place, has not been achieved by pressing still more closely together those who live under crowded conditions ; on the contrary, the pressure and crowding are shown to be markedly diminished. There has been improvement in the quality as well as increase in the quantity of wage-earners' houses.

It is a fair inference from these facts that voluntary enterprise is able to act as efficiently in the future as in the past, and that the improvement in the housing of the people will continue, if the impulses which have led to it be not checked. The following are the facts, taken from the Census of England and Wales, 1901, County of London, which lead to these conclusions. The references are to the published Census.

During the ten years 1891—1901 the population of the administrative County of

London showed an increase of 308,000 (Summary, p. ix., Table 1, p. 1).

In the City of London, however, and six of the central metropolitan boroughs[1] there was an actual decline of 67,000 (Summary, pp. ix. and x., Table 9 and 9A, pp. 14—22).

A transference of population, therefore, took place from these central boroughs to other districts. Fresh house-room was, therefore, provided during the decade in the County of London for 375,000 persons.

Large as is this figure, it is dwarfed by the increase which took place during the decade in the Greater London of the Metropolitan and City police district, which includes portions of the counties of Surrey, Kent, Essex and Hertford (Table 22B, p. 64).

In Greater London the Census shows an increase of no less than 947,000, consisting of 308,000 within the County of London, and 639,000 without the county. To this figure 947,000 must be added the 67,000 due to the transference of population within the County of London. The total number

[1] Viz., Bermondsey, Finsbury, Holborn, St. Marylebone, Shoreditch, and City of Westminster.

of those for whom additional house-room was provided during the decade was 1,014,000.

The amount of capital sunk in providing this accommodation is a matter of conjecture. Reckoning the family at 4·4 persons on an average (Summary, p. x.), the number of families housed was 230,000. At a capital expenditure of £250 a family, the sum expended exceeds £57,000,000.

It appears from the Returns published by the London County Council to March 31st, 1902 (Housing Manager's Tables A and D), that the Council has provided accommodation to that date for 15,000 persons, and that the population of the buildings according to a census taken on December 31st, 1901, was 10,719. It further appears by the same Returns (Return IV., pp. 10—16), that the Council has expended on buildings completed upon March 31st, 1901, £1,281,000. It may be observed that in this estimate of expenditure the cost of the sites is not the actual cost price, but a figure estimated as the value of the land restricted to the purpose of housing the working classes. Reckoning the family at 4·4 persons on an average, the

Council has spent in housing each family according to the higher rate of population £374, and according to the lower rate of population £525.

In proportion to the wage-earning population of London, the number of persons housed by the Council, 10,000, is inconsiderable. It may further be noticed that not a few of the buildings, as for instance on the Boundary Street estate, have been erected by the Council in districts in which the population has remained stationary during the decade, as will be afterwards more particularly explained. The houses, therefore, which the Council has built in these districts do not form part of the great excess in accommodation which has been provided since 1891 for 1,014,000 persons.

This work, therefore, has, with insignificant exceptions, been done by voluntary commercial enterprise.

It seems impossible, in the face of such facts and figures as these, to maintain that the business of providing house-room is moribund; on the contrary, commercial enterprise as applied to house-building has shown marked signs of activity and of growth.

It may be noticed for what it is worth that the houses in course of erection in the County of London in 1891 were 4,194, and 4,624 in 1901, an increase of 10·3 per cent. (Summary, p. x., Table 1, p. 1).

The Census returns, moreover, make it clear that the increase in the number of persons housed has not been gained by packing people still more closely together; on the contrary, the houses of the people are distinctly less crowded than they were ten years ago. The rate of increase of population in the County of London during the decade was 7·3 (Summary, p. ix.). "The total number of separate tenements," to quote from the Summary, p. x., "which had been 937,006 in 1891, rose to 1,019,546, the increase being equal to 8·7 per cent. Of this total the tenements containing five or more rooms increased from 307,037 to 347,516, equal to 13·2 per cent.; while the increase of those with less than five rooms was from 630,569 to 672,030, and did not exceed 6·6 per cent. The rate of increase in the larger tenements was, therefore, exactly double that shown in the smaller tenements. Stated in another way, the tenements with five or more rooms were equal to 32.7 per cent. of the total tenements in 1891, and to 34.1 per cent. at the recent Census—while the percentage of the tenements with less than five rooms declined from 67.3 to 65.9. The reduction in the number of the latter class of tenements was most strongly marked in the tenements of one room, which declined from 172,502 in 1891 to 149,524—that is, from 18.4 per cent. of the total tenements, to 14.7 per cent. It may further be pointed out that the number of single-roomed tenements in which more than two persons were enumerated declined from 56,622 to 40,762."

It further appears from a consideration of Table 19, p. 58, that the number of single-roomed tenements in which more than three persons were enumerated declined from 27,617 to 17,082.

Again, the number of tenements of two rooms in which more than four persons were enumerated declined from 54,872 to 50,304, and the number of tenements of three rooms in which more than seven persons were enumerated declined from 12,571 to 11,953.

Table 19 has so strong a bearing on the condition of the poor of London as to house-room that it is printed in the Appendix, p. 115, of this volume.

The spreading out of population evidenced by Table 19 implies that more rooms are used to accommodate the same number of persons. Where are the new houses? The Census returns give a clear answer. The increase in population in the County of London has taken place mainly in the districts near the border of the county, on land not previously built upon. Thus, as appears from a consideration of Table 12, pp. 27—37, in the registration districts of Fulham, Wandsworth, Lambeth (sub-districts 6 and 7), Camberwell (sub-districts 1 and 2), and Lewisham (sub-districts 3 and 4), the population has risen from 748,000 to 973,000, showing an increase of 225,000, which is at the rate of 30 per cent. The rest of the County of London has only increased in population by 2·3 per cent. In an immense continuous area of Central London, containing 1,280,000 people, the population was during the decade either declining or stationary.[1] This area consists of the City of London and the boroughs of St. Pancras, St. Marylebone, Westminster, Chelsea, Bermondsey, Bethnal Green, Shoreditch, Finsbury, and Holborn. With these may be included sub-districts 1, 2, and 3 of the registration district of Southwark, and sub-districts 1 and 2 of the registration district of Lambeth.

There is a further point to be noted. There has been during the period 1891—1901 a large amount of rebuilding in London. New buildings have taken the place of old insanitary property, while existing houses have been largely renovated and improved. These changes are of great importance. There can be no doubt, for example, that the 50,304 families consisting of more than four persons, who are still, unfortunately, living in tenements of two rooms, are housed under more healthy conditions than the

[1] Bethnal Green shows an increase of 751, Chelsea of 888, and St. Pancras of 568; these may, therefore, fairly be classed as stationary.

54,872 similar families of the preceding Census. The history of the East End Dwellings Company furnishes an illustration. Since 1891 the company has spent more than £200,000 in erecting new buildings for wage-earners in districts in which the population has during the decade either declined or remained stationary. The effect of the company's work has been to substitute new and better for old and worse accommodation.

These various considerations show that voluntary enterprise has been active during the decade, both in providing new and additional house-room for an immense increase of population, and also in substituting new and improved dwellings for the old insanitary houses.

It is not true, therefore, as is alleged by some advocates of State intervention, that commercial enterprise is moribund and unable to provide houses for the people. It has done a great work and effected a vast improvement in the homes of wage-earners, and will continue to work, though the intervention of the State, if effected as is proposed, will tend to impair its efficiency.

It is indeed quite possible, as will subsequently appear, that the assumption of responsibility by the State may result in causing a loss, and not a gain, in the number of houses erected for wage-earners. The competition of the State, whether or not it be really formidable in the particular case of house-building, is much feared, and may easily produce a withdrawal of voluntary enterprise from the field more than equal in value to its own contribution.

CHAPTER III.

CONDITIONS OF EFFICIENCY.

A CONSIDERATION of the achievements of free enterprise in providing the houses needed to accommodate the great increase of population leads on to an examination of the characteristics required to secure efficiency in the work. What are the conditions of improvement ? London and other large cities, considered as places of residence, exhibit traits which inspire misgiving. They are lacking in the ample supply of pure air and the companionship of the natural world—its sights, sounds and odours —which keep body and mind sound and wholesome. The insufficiency of cities in these respects has been long noted and deplored. Yet still men rush to them ; the attraction is too strong. They are the seats of manufacture, the centres of trade ; they are hives of industry and activity. In them

wages are higher, and the choice of work
and of friends is wider. In them there is
more to gratify the taste, more to interest
and excite the mind. Cities, too, are the
resort of those who adopt an unsettled way
of life by necessity or by choice, or who are
broken down in fortune or in reputation.
Whatever of praise or of blame be due to life
in cities, it seems wiser to recognise the facts
and to make the best of them rather than to
maintain an unequal struggle against them.
These disquieting features in civic life are
symptoms of human activity and of human
needs. They represent impulses which, like
the waters of a river, it is more profitable to
guide than to oppose.

The pressure of population in cities touches
the entire life of those who reside or work in
them. The narrow conditions of the town
compare unfavourably with the amplitude of
the country. Economy of space demands
sacrifices which affect the size, style, and
surroundings of the home. Whatever, moreover, be the case in the country, dwellings in
towns are built as an investment of capital
on which a sufficient return is expected.

The efficiency of a building depends on a suitable compromise being effected between the interests of the owner and the occupier, which will vary in its terms with the place and with the circumstances, but which will always bear the impress of its origin in the stress of life in cities. The architect and manager will show their art in making the compromise as beneficial as possible to both parties. It is important that the occupier should get a healthy home suitable to his requirements and to his income. It is also important that the owner should receive such a return on his investment as will attract fresh capital into the business as opportunity offers. The problem is not a simple one. The business is unlike the supply of gas or water, the carriage of persons or goods, or the delivery of letters. In such matters the same acts are performed for whomsoever they are undertaken. But in the matter of housing wage-earners, differences in the income, habits, and tastes of occupiers demand differences in the homes supplied to them. It is clear, therefore, that experience, resourcefulness and patience are needed in order to search for and find the arrangements which will secure the stability and growth of the business in the interests alike of the owners, the occupiers, and the ever-increasing number of those who require a wide choice of suitable accommodation.

The complexities involved will stand out more clearly when the subject is further considered from the point of view of the occupiers of the houses and from the point of view of those who provide them.

The first broad fact about the occupiers is that they are persons of very different incomes and very different requirements as regards their homes. Artisans who earn 40s. to 50s. a week need a different style of accommodation from that suitable to a labourer earning 20s. to 30s. a week.

Moreover, even if the wage-earner's income be the same, the claims on him may be different. The couple with six children require more house-room than a childless pair; while there is indefinite variation in the charges on income due to sickness, the support of parents and other special circumstances. Beside differences in income and

in the claims on income, there are wide
variations in habits, in the standard of living,
and in skill in the management of income.
Some people, though in receipt of good
wages, seem always to be in difficulties;
others, earning lower wages, seem always
comfortable.   Some, unhappily, have a
standard of living which is below their
surroundings—their rooms, though good, are
dirty and ill kept; others rise above their
surroundings—the home is an oasis in a
squalid street.

These differences in the circumstances of
wage-earners give rise to a demand for
differences in the size, style and arrangement
of houses.   There cannot be too great variety
in the accommodation offered.   No one who
has undertaken house-hunting on his own
account can have any doubt on the matter.

The need of variety in accommodation
may be urged from another point of view.
House-room is one of many requirements of
each family.   Employment, by which the
income is won, food, clothing, and fuel,
protection against the risks due to sickness,
old age, and death, the education of children,

these and other needs compete with house-room as claims on the wage-earner. Each and all of these requirements are governed by the wage-earner's standard of living; there is an interdependence between them; the multitudinous facts which concern each man and each family form a group which differs from every other group. No two men have the same life-story.

It is improper, therefore, to separate any one of these requirements from its position in the group, and to consider it as if it existed alone and apart from the standard of living which affects each and every detail of the wage-earner's life. There is need to find the true perspective which embraces the whole field.

No item of the family requirements lends itself more readily to separate consideration and treatment than the home. It is in view; it is always there; a defect in it, whether in quantity or quality, offends or alarms a person of cultivated sanitary sense. There is a strong temptation to isolate this particular item from the group of family requirements, and to expect people to attain a standard of living as regards their house-room which they do not attain in other respects. No attempt to deal with the home out of its true perspective will yield a satis-factory result. An example may be permitted. An owner, inspired by the idea that no family ought to live in one room only, visits the occupiers of his house. He finds two families living side by side, each in one room. One occupier consumes in drink or gambling the money which might provide a second room; the other occupier, a widow of good character, earns the full wages current in her trade, and is just able by a struggle to maintain herself and her children in independence. The deficiency in house-room is caused in the one case by immoral habits, for which the occupier is responsible; it is caused in the other case by scantiness of earnings, for which the occupier is not responsible. Will any reasonable man include these two occupiers in the same sentence of condemna-tion?—at least, if he be a man who values independence and respects those who strive to maintain it?

The judgment which suggests itself in

these cases is clear enough so far as the cause of the overcrowding is concerned. As regards the amount of overcrowding, there is room for legitimate difference of opinion. It may become a duty to endure a certain amount of overcrowding when the income cannot be enlarged and when the extra cost of increased accommodation will entail the loss of things reasonably necessary to the well-being of the family.

It may possibly be urged that the housing of the people may fairly receive special and separate treatment if it be specially unsatisfactory. This plea, whatever it may be worth, does not apply to the present condition of wage-earners in London. Their homes are better in every way at the present time than they were ever before, and they are, as has been shown, improving. The present outcry, indeed, implies that the standard of requirement is rising with respect to them. Wage-earners in London are not in a worse position as regards their houseroom than as regards their clothing or their nourishment. In all these items improvement is greatly to be desired, but not more in the matter of housing than in other particulars.

It may further be urged that the supply of houses may fairly receive special treatment because it is undertaken under special difficulty owing to the limited space available and to the laws and customs which regulate the tenure and transfer of land. The answer to such a contention is two-fold. Notwithstanding these difficulties, voluntary enterprise has succeeded, as has been shown, in providing house-room in surprising quantities. It seems better, moreover, to endeavour to lessen the difficulties by simplifying, so far as possible, our laws and arrangements concerning land. The more completely land is brought under the influence of free exchange the less formidable will these difficulties become, and the less will be the temptation to treat the supply of house-room differently from the supply of the other requirements of civilized living.

The further, indeed, the matter is probed, the clearer appears the error of isolating any one of the items which make up the sum of human needs. The particular defect, a

result of poverty, or ignorance, or misconduct, will only be made good if labour
become more productive, or knowledge be
increased, or character be improved. These
beneficial changes are more likely to be
delayed than hastened if consideration be
limited to the particular need without regard
to the whole group of requirements of which
it is a part.

From the occupier's point of view, then,
there is need of as great variety as possible
in the capacity and equipment of tenements
at a corresponding variety of rent, in order
to meet variety in circumstances; nor can
approval be given to any attempt to treat the
home out of its true position in the family
budget as one of many requirements.

It is time to consider the matter from the
owner's point of view.

Whatever may have been the case in times
past, or may be the case elsewhere, it seems
plain that the supply of new or improved
houses for wage-earners in the more central
districts of London will be provided for the
occupants by owners who have built them as
an investment of capital.

Houses in London are not ancillary to any industry. Rentals in country districts are often so low that cottages for labourers may fairly be considered as adjuncts of the business of agriculture, as part of the plant necessary to carry it on. The owner receives his return, partially at all events, in the low scale of remuneration given to those who work on the land. The labourer on the land is paid partly in wages, partly in the cheapness of his house and garden.

The fulfilment of the owner's expectation that a suitable return will be earned is the best, indeed the only guarantee, that the means of providing fresh houses will be forthcoming as the need from time to time arises. The profit which it is possible to earn, due regard being paid to the welfare of the occupiers, may not be large ; but it is, as experience has shown, better secured than in some forms of investment to which capital is freely attracted. The more completely house property is regarded as an investment of capital, the more will the owners prefer security to a high immediate return; the more will they build their houses solidly, and spend thought and ingenuity in

making them healthy, well arranged, and suitable homes for their tenants.

Investments are, speaking generally, secure in proportion as they are concerned with the ordinary requirements of large masses of people. The broader the basis of a business, the less is it exposed to the changes and chances of fashion. One element of instability is held in check. The provision of dwellings meets a very ordinary requirement. It is well, however, to remember that the full benefit of the position will not be secured unless the owner has freedom to adapt the commodity which he supplies to the needs of those who demand it. The need of freedom from external restraint is common to all businesses which depend for success upon a ready adaptability to the changing wants of the customers. Such freedom is particularly necessary in the business of building houses, because the material of which the house is built is unchanging; the requisite adaptations, therefore, must be made beforehand in the minds of those who design them. Great indeed is the responsibility of the man who builds a house. It has a quality and a magnetism of its own; such as it is, it remains; it cannot, like a house of cards, be knocked down and rebuilt at will; it attracts those congenial to it, and keeps them at its own level; it is an instrument in the formation of character.

The owner, therefore, who aspires to efficiency in his work needs to make constant efforts towards improvement in design and in detail, in order to provide a wide range of choice, to meet the ever-rising standard of requirement and to make the houses the best possible, having regard to the means and circumstances of the probable occupiers. The uses of mobility are not confined to war. Success in peaceful competition attends those who are adaptable, ingenious, and ever open to new ideas. These qualities are the sources of efficiency and of improvement in house-building as in other human affairs.

Efforts after efficiency and improvement, it may be noted, are not always most usefully directed to an increase of elaboration and expense, as it is a mistake to provide dwellings which those who need them most cannot or will not occupy.

This difficulty—the adaptation of supply to demand—is inherent in the business, and must be faced by any one who aspires to conduct it efficiently.

After the capital has been provided, the houses designed and built, and the occupiers have entered at a suitable rent, the property has to be managed. It is likely that, in the central districts at all events, the buildings will be on the "block" plan—*i.e.*, where the outside walls, roof, staircases and other things are common to a number of tenements. Where the occupiers are living so near each other and have much in common, the comfort of all depends on the behaviour of each. It is clearly in the owner's interest that the building should be attractive to a good class of occupier. It is, therefore, needful that care be exercised in the selection of occupiers, the enforcement of order and cleanliness, and the prevention of overcrowding. The manager must also check waste while keeping the buildings in good repair; good management, therefore, needs a combination of qualities not always easy to secure.

It is plain, from the considerations which have been urged, that the interests of owners and occupiers unite in demanding certain conditions of efficiency in the work of providing houses. The profits of the business need to be sufficient to secure its growth; insight, ingenuity, and power of management are required in order to adapt the houses to the varying requirements of the tenants; moreover, a certain reasonable freedom from restraint is needed in order that these qualities may bear their proper fruit.

CHAPTER IV.

STORY OF A BUILDING COMPANY.

In order to illustrate the foregoing considerations, it is now proposed to give a
short account of the work of the East End
Dwellings Company, Limited.   It is not
claimed that there is anything special in
the history of the company.   It is, therefore, the more valuable as an illustration.

The East End of London was in 1883,
and indeed still is, in the main a city of
cottages, situate for the most part in good
streets, sometimes, however, in narrow close
courts, structurally designed each to be the
home of one family, but now too often overcrowded and defective from a sanitary point
of view.   Block dwellings also existed, some
of them erected and managed on a commercial basis, and inhabited by well-to-do
artisans.   The buildings erected under the
Peabody Trust housed a certain number of

poorer persons, but there was no provision on a commercial basis for the poorer class of respectable workpeople other than the tenement houses which have been mentioned.

In this state of things it was felt that these poorer folk would receive great benefit by the provision of dwellings of which the design and the management should be favourable to good health and good character; it was thought, too, that the necessary business relations with the tenants might be made the opportunity of bringing civilising influence to bear on them. In carrying out the work it was deemed essential to pay due regard to the pressure of population to centres, and no less essential to make the affair a commercial success—*i.e.*, yield such a return as would attract capital into the business, and so extend automatically better accommodation for the poor as opportunity might arise.

These ideas were developed in two ways: according to one method, exemplified in the work of Miss Octavia Hill and of the Tenement Dwellings Company, existing houses were acquired, put into repair, and managed in such a way as to influence the tenants for good; according to the other method, the site was acquired and specially designed dwellings were built upon it. It was the latter work which the East End Dwellings Company undertook. There is ample scope for both methods, and no inconsistency whatever between their aims. The firstfruits of the company's work was the erection in 1885 of Katharine Buildings, Aldgate, near the Royal Mint. The plans were laid before the highest authorities among those in personal touch with the poor. The prevailing ideas were that publicity should be courted, that the fittings should be of the simplest in view of the destructive habits of the tenants, the buildings airy and wholesome, and the rents low. These objects were attained to the fullest extent. The building consists of a ground floor and four stories with balconies; the latrines are in groups on the landings; the block is 30 feet deep and contains 285 rooms in nests of five rooms, one of which is small. More than 200 of the rooms were constructed to be let each as a separate

tenement. The erection of Lolesworth
Buildings, Spitalfields, followed in 1886—a
block almost as large and very similar in
design, excepting that the latrines are not
upon the landing, the unsuitability of this
position becoming at once apparent.

These buildings were, and are, managed
by a lady manager, who has caretakers under
her and directs the ordinary repairs. She is
assisted by other ladies responsible to her.
The principles of management are important.
The would-be tenant is seen by the lady
manager and visited at his previous home
by the caretaker; no person is admitted of
criminal or immoral habits or of obvious
unsuitability; payment of rent, orderly
conduct, and as little overcrowding as
possible are insisted upon. It was thought
that buildings so managed would benefit the
tenants in health and in character; they
would live in well-drained, airy, and spacious
dwellings, and would be subject to the dis-
cipline involved in the necessity for orderly
conduct and the regular payment of rent, and
in such associated action as the use of the
common laundry; they would, moreover, be

brought under the cultured influence of the lady manager and her assistants.

The experience gained on these two blocks soon disclosed the difficulties of building for the very poor only. The greater the publicity, the more do the acts and defaults of the less civilised affect the comfort of all. It is difficult for the tenants of these large blocks to rise above a certain standard of living unless all are well behaved—a condition difficult to secure in a population of those who inhabit one room, and are often " casual " in their occupations, earnings, and habits. The success of such a block, therefore, depends wholly on the management. Unsuitability in either the manager or the caretaker may cause failure, both as regards the good of the tenants and the finances of the company.

This experience and these considerations determined the company to include in their scope provision for more highly paid work-people.

Museum Building, in Bethnal Green, accordingly, is a composite block of shops, self-contained flats, and single rooms; it is managed on a different plan—viz., by a resident superintendent.

The Cromer Street Estate, King's Cross, built in 1891—3, consists of several blocks, some composed of self-contained flats, and some on the associated plan for poorer tenants. A crucial experiment was here made as to the relative cost of balconies and inside staircases. Two blocks opposite each other were tendered for at the same time; the balcony block was 28 feet deep, the inside staircase block 30 feet. The latter, to the general surprise, proved the cheaper. This experiment determined the company to discard the balcony plan, and thereby gain both in privacy and economy.

Cressy Houses, Stepney Green, built in 1894, showed an important development in such matters as the number of rooms in the tenement, the fittings, fireplaces, and wash-houses. It had become apparent that the standard of requirement in the dwellings of working people was rising.

In Pollard Houses, Pentonville, erected in 1895, a great improvement was introduced. One room in each story is used as a washhouse for the joint use of four tenements. The plan has been liked wherever adopted, and no difficulty has been experienced in getting the slightly increased rent required. The company, with some trepidation, built a very large block on this plan close to the new buildings of the London County Council on the Boundary Street area, Bethnal Green. The success was complete; the buildings filled at once and are popular. The other dwellings belonging to the company call for no remark.

The company have long wished to build cottages, or cottage flats, in London, and some time ago made an offer for a site adapted to the purpose, but were not successful in securing it. The rise which has taken place in the cost of building is not favourable to the success of such an experiment.

In this brief account structural and financial detail has been avoided; it may, however, be useful to add some remarks on the design and management of buildings.

Even as regards the immediate future, the planning of a new building involves complex considerations, such as the capacity of the site as regards building space, vacant space, light, and air; the need for such a building, having regard to the pressure of population, existing accommodation, and rents current in the neighbourhood; perhaps most difficult of all—the type or types of tenement likely to prove most attractive. The company provide three types:—(1) the self-contained flat, suitable for the more well-to-do; (2) the single room, for people of small income; (3) an intermediate type, consisting of two or even three rooms, with use of closet and washhouse jointly with others. This last plan has certain advantages of its own; the rent of such a three-roomed tenement is much the same as the rent of a flat containing two rooms, scullery, and closet, while the tenant gains a living room, which may be of importance to decency and well-being when the family is growing up; the two last types, moreover, have the advantage that there is no inlet from the sewer inside the tenement, and that the closets are subject to the inspection and control of the managers and superintendent.

It is, furthermore, wise not to lose sight of the possibility of development in a more remote future; reference has been made to the rising standard of requirement in workmen's homes; nor should the future be sacrificed to the present by the erection of dwellings which minister to the physical health rather than to the moral advancement of their inhabitants. It will be noted that the company's buildings show a distinct development of design, becoming more and more suited to be the homes of healthy and civilised people.

However much skill be shown in selecting sites and in designing and erecting buildings, the success of the enterprise depends upon the management by those who direct the whole undertaking as well as by those who are set over the several dwellings. It is surprising how many matters of difficulty arise in an affair so apparently simple as the letting of unfurnished tenements.

Structural improvements will claim the directors' attention in matters great and small, from the alteration of a sanitary system to the piercing of a wall between two rooms.

A very important part of the directors'
work consists in the selection of those who
are to be in actual contact with the tenants.
To these managers and superintendents
are entrusted the selection of tenants, the
enforcement of punctual payment of rent and
of orderly conduct, and the responsibility
for arrangements for the cleanliness of yards,
staircases, passages and closets which are
common to two or more tenements. The
temper and spirit in which affairs are
managed make all the difference to the
utility of the buildings as a place of residence
where respectable tenants may live in contentment, and where undisciplined tenants
may be brought under the steadying influence which they need. However excellent
the managers and superintendents may be,
experience shows that the directors should
be frequent in their visits to the several
buildings, and careful in their inspection
of them. They should be in touch with
the managers and superintendents on the
various matters on which well-being depends;
they should sympathise with their subordin-
ates in the difficulties which are sure to

arise, and give ear to the proposals which practical experience suggests ; they should, above all, use their influence towards the maintenance of a high standard of management as regards cleanliness, order and just dealings with the tenants.

The East End Dwellings Company manage their buildings either by a lady manager, or by a resident superintendent, or by a division of responsibility between the superintendent and a rent-collector. The method of management, however, is of less importance than the personal qualities of the managers ; even the same manager may be more successful with one class of tenant than with another. The manager should be firm, just, and genial, with a strong insight into human character, and a power of adaptation which will make his or her sway at once disciplinary and attractive.

It is worth while to dwell for a moment on this matter of management. The lower in the social scale is the class of tenant to be housed, the more important and the more difficult does the management become. A group of self-contained flats occupied by well-to-do people requires little management. But well-to-do people are not those whose condition as to house-room needs improvement the most. The poorer part of labouring folk find it their interest for cheapness' sake to live in association with others. The closer the association the more necessary are such qualities as cleanly habits, a sense of order, and tact and temper to bear and to forbear. The exercise of these qualities implies a considerable advance in the arts of civilised living. The class, therefore, which has had the least opportunity of advancement in these arts is just the class which needs them most. Residence in a well-managed building affords an opportunity of such advancement in several ways. Insistence on the punctual payment of rent, and on orderly and cleanly conduct, induces such as are undisciplined to look one step beyond the present, and to control the impulses which make for destitution, violence, and squalor. Good management, too, gives a practical illustration of the results in comfort and contentment which flow from conduct which is reasonable, tolerant, and conciliatory.

Good management, moreover, affords an opportunity for the growth of some kind of healthy public feeling among the tenants. It inspires confidence between man and man, and tends to mitigate the distrust which deems each man's hand to be against every other man.

It is at first sight somewhat singular to find that the successful conduct of a business affair requires the exercise of an educative personal influence. This influence, however, is the means of securing the loyal and whole-hearted co-operation on the part of all concerned which is needed in order to secure the best results in all forms of associated effort.

The healthiness of the company's buildings has been very satisfactory. During the four years 1898—1901, on a population rising from 4,800 to 6,000, the death rates, including those removed to hospital, were 13·32, 15·39, 13·98, 12·63, or an average of 13·83 per 1,000. These rates compare with the rates for all London in the three earlier years of 18·2, 19·3, 18·3, or an average of 18·6 per 1,000. Nor does this favourable result follow from any disproportionate lack of young couples with families; the birth rates in the same four years were 32, 35·73, 29·11, 33·20, or an average of 32·53 per 1,000. These rates compare with the rates for all London in the three earlier years of 29·4, 29·7, 28·6, or an average of 29·2 per 1,000.

It may be mentioned that the East End Dwellings Company in 1901 housed in their various buildings more than 6,000 persons, at the rate of 647 to the acre, after allowing one half of the public thoroughfares adjoining the buildings. Such a population to the acre is not exceptional. The report of the Peabody Trustees for the same year states that they have a population of 19,000, at the rate of 700 to the acre. These rates are far in excess of those obtaining in the most crowded parts of London, according to the recent Census. Some instances are the following :—

Name.		Area.	Population.	No. per acre.	Reference in Census.
Whitechapel	...	Registration district	78,768	214	p. 34
Spitalfields	...	Sub-district	27,969	331	p. 34
St. Andrew's, Holborn	...	Parish	25,103	213	p. 30
Shoreditch	...	District	118,637	183	p. 33
Bethnal Green	...	,,	129,680	170	p. 33
St. Giles	...		31,436	135	p. 29

It is true that the dwellings belonging to the East End Dwellings Company and to the Peabody Trustees are not contiguous ; the Census, moreover, does not give the proportion of the several areas which is used for residential purposes. There is no desire, therefore, to press any argument based on these figures. They suggest, however, that a large district, such as Bethnal Green, which is chiefly residential in character, may, without sanitary disadvantage, accommodate an increased population by the gradual substitution of new and improved houses for the small cottages which at present largely occupy the ground.

The East End Dwellings Company have expended more than £340,000 in buildings, and have for many years paid a dividend of £5 per cent. upon the ordinary share capital.

The total cost of house property to the owner consists of two ingredients—the cost of the site and the cost of the building. While the cost of the buildings and the charges on them on the one hand, and the current rentals on the other, stand at the

present figures, it is commercially impracticable to give more than a certain price
for the site. The nearer the site lies to
centres of commercial activity, the higher
is its price in the open market. This increase in value implies that the land is useful
for the purposes of trade; it is an instrument in the manufacture or distribution of
commodities.

The Summary of the Census, p. ix., states:
" In the City of London and six of the central
metropolitan boroughs the enumerated population showed an actual decline of over
67,000 in the ten years, notwithstanding that
the recorded excess of births over deaths in
that period amounted approximately to
70,000. In the central boroughs, with one
exception, a decrease of population has
regularly occurred during the last four
intercensal periods, and has been due in
a great measure to the transformation of
dwelling houses into warehouses, offices,
and business premises. This centrifugal
dispersion of town population is, however,
shared by all great, old, and prosperous
cities."

It is rarely advantageous to fight against an economic tendency. It is not surprising, therefore, that the reservation for dwellings of sites which have a high value in the open market is now generally admitted to be mistaken. Such reservation, moreover, is superfluous, as at no great distance sites suitable for dwelling houses can usually be found. The finding of sites, indeed, is among the least of the difficulties of the business.

There exists in London a large amount of cottage property which is old and ripe for demolition. The substitution of larger and better houses for those which are small and insanitary will give wage-earners better homes and more of them. The rate at which the substitution takes place depends upon the rate at which the old dilapidated property falls in ; it is clearly impracticable to demolish cottages which have still plenty of life in them, even though they may not be of a design suitable to accommodate the number of families now contained in them.

There is a further point which may be noted. Many of those who are living under crowded conditions in central districts cannot, or can no longer, show reasons for their residence connected with their employment. They are attached to the spot or the neighbourhood by habit, the proximity of friends, or the allurements of endowed or voluntary charity. Municipal buildings which house people at less than the commercial rate will exercise a similar attraction. The attempt to make a distinction between the occupiers based on the urgency or genuineness of the reasons for their residence would be invidious and impracticable. It is natural to sympathise with those who experience the inconveniences which arise from residence under narrow and crowded conditions. It seems more reasonable, however, to treat the matter as one of the changes and chances of life to which all classes of the community are subject, and which forms no sufficient ground for the special intervention of the State.

In the cost of building a considerable increase has occurred of late years. The value of labour and materials has risen in the aggregate 20 per cent. since the year

1893. Part of this increase represents the fair share of the building trade in the general prosperity; but part is due to the action of wage-earners and their unions, with which it is impossible to sympathise. No reasonable person will complain that honest work should receive a full, even a generous, reward; but there seems to be a just ground of complaint when, as in the case of bricklayers, a far smaller amount of work is done in exchange for good wages than is reasonable. The more energetic workmen are not permitted to reap the reward of superior energy, and the cost of building is increased not only by the extra amount paid in wages, but by the numerous charges which accumulate when building is dilatory. It may be thought that this evil will cure itself, and that workmen will be compelled to maintain a fair standard of work under the penalty of losing it altogether. It must, however, be remembered that the erection of workmen's dwellings is only one branch of the building trade, which has been as a whole in a state of such activity for many years that the workmen have been able to act as they please in this respect. It is only fair to bear in mind, when increased rents are complained of, that a substantial ingredient in the increase is to be found in the enhanced cost of building caused by the action of the workmen and their unions.

It must not, however, be supposed that the increased cost of building has in point of fact made it impracticable to conduct the business to a satisfactory profit, as the experience of the East End Dwellings Company testifies. The published accounts of the company show that on a capital expenditure of £131,000 incurred between 1893 and 1900, the net return in 1901 was £5 7s. per cent.

In considering the suitability of workmen's dwellings for the investment of capital, it is fair to include a period of years in the review. The attractiveness of the investment varies from time to time according to the rate of return yielded by other securities or enterprises which compete with it for the favour of investors. When capital is plentiful and the rate of interest is low, an investment which yields a moderate return is naturally more sought after than when capital is scarce and the rate of interest is high.

It is desired to reiterate that this account of the East End Dwellings Company has been given as an illustration simply because the author has had personal experience of its management. Voluntary enterprise in house-building assumes many forms. The commercial company may not be the most typical method of its working. The private owner and the speculative builder doubtless exceed the commercial company in the extent of their several operations. It seems probable, however, that sooner or later those who have capital at their command, if they be not frightened by the competition of the State, will awake to the opportunities of secure investment which the business of housing wage-earners affords. Such investments will then take the place among recognised securities to which their intrinsic worth entitles them.

CHAPTER V.

INEFFICIENCY OF MUNICIPAL BUILDING.

IN the course of the previous discussion grounds have been given for the belief that voluntary enterprise is both able and willing, if unchecked, to continue its activity in providing improved houses for people in London. The conditions have also been set forth which tend towards the efficient conduct of the business in the interest of both occupiers and owners. It remains to examine the influence which the contemplated intervention of the councils is likely to exert upon the supply of houses. Are the houses of wage-earners likely to become, through the labours of the councils, more in quantity and better in quality?

Voluntary commercial enterprise achieves the beneficial result of supplying people with such things as they are willing to pay for. This result is none the less beneficial because it is in order to earn a profit for himself that a man of business works. It is the mutuality of benefit received by the parties to a bargain which gives to industry and commerce a special value in the social order. Difficulties and dangers beset the paths of those who, in the political world, seek to force their will on others, or, in the charitable world, confer the means of living on those who offer no equivalent. From these perils the man of business is exempt. Business consists in a free exchange of good offices.

The motive power which brings about this exchange of services is the desire of each party to the bargain to serve his own interest. It works, therefore, in accord with the normal action of human nature. It does not wax or wane with the enthusiasms of the hour ; there is no need of an agitation to secure it. Its action is indirect and automatic. The demand for commodities acts as a continuing inducement to those who find a profit in supplying them.

There is a further point. Commercial men compete against each other for the favour of their customers. Their success, ' indeed their continued existence as men of business, depends on their efficiency. Voluntary enterprise has become a school in which the prizes fall to those who show integrity and industry as well as ingenuity and skill. So well have the lessons been learnt, and so efficiently does the economic machine work, that no effort of politicians or philanthropists could anticipate the varying needs of the people with the certainty and the elasticity displayed by men of business.

Commercial enterprise, then, considered as an instrument for the supply of commodities, has well-marked traits. It acts through a free exchange of services, working with certainty and elasticity; it offers guarantees for the continuance of its good offices; it promotes efficiency and the personal qualities which conduce to efficiency.

The previous discussion has made it clear that these traits have been conspicuously manifested by voluntary enterprise in the work of providing houses for wage-earners. The State, however, stands in a very different position. It is doubtful whether there ever is a true mutuality, or free exchange of services, between the State and a subject. However this may be, the motive power behind the State's action is wholly different from the inducements which prompt voluntary enterprise. The State undertakes the work in order to meet an assumed public need, and not in order to earn a profit. It may, indeed, be right that the State should submit to a loss in order to achieve the desired result.

Important consequences follow from this difference in motive power. The energy displayed by the State in the work will depend upon the degree of pressure which the public, and especially the ratepayers, continue to exercise on those whom they elect to serve on the councils. Popular enthusiasm, however, is fickle. It is easy to impose responsibility for action on a public body; it is still easier to leave it to repose there, when other claims are made upon public energy and the public purse. The State acts impulsively at the instigation of those who from time to time are in the ascendant. Voluntary enterprise acts automatically according to the prospects which appear of conducting business to a satisfactory issue. The State, then, lacks the continuing inducement to action with which the desire to earn a profit inspires voluntary enterprise.

But this is not all. Boundless possibilities of inefficiency are opened out when men attempt to dispense with the motives which are the appropriate spurs to human endeavour. An increase in the usefulness of dwellings can only be secured by an increase of knowledge of the varied requirements of wage-earners, and an increase of skill in giving effect to this knowledge. There is little reason to augur that those who manage on behalf of the State will exhibit an increase of knowledge and of skill. The pressure on them of competition, the greatest of all spurs to improvement, will be reduced to a minimum. The guarantee of the rates will be ever at hand. They will be more than human if they do not become satisfied with their handiwork and averse to striving after improvement. There will, moreover, necessarily arise an immense system equipped with officials, machinery, regulations, and precedents. A mass of obstruction will thus be formed, difficult to approach and hard to move. The condition of the public services is instructive. The navy and the army are of vital importance to the nation: they are not wholly free from the spur of competition, as they have before them the example of foreign powers. It is nevertheless a common complaint that in the management of the services officialism and inertness gather into an obstructive mass, which the stimulus of a great war is needed to overcome. What similar incentive will be found to stimulate a Housing Department? Such influences, moreover, as reach the department are not likely to make for improvement. Control will probably be exercised by persons who have fixed ideas on the matter of housing, and treat it apart from the general condition of the persons to be housed. Houses will not be built to suit the occupiers; occupiers will be expected to adjust themselves to houses. The dwellings, even if they embody much that is excellent in design, are likely to be planned by those who have little knowledge of the varied requirements of wage-earners, and small incentive to exercise ingenuity in meeting them. The larger the scale of the public building operations and the longer continued the public efforts, the greater is likely to be the inefficiency displayed in adapting the houses to the requirements of the occupiers.

Furthermore, the officials employed by the State are unlikely to display efficiency in management, especially in the case of buildings tenanted by the poorer class of labourers. Such officials can hardly be expected to give the detailed attention and to exert the personal influence which are indispensable in order to obtain the best results. It is significant that the buildings of the London County Council appear to be designed in order to house a class of tenant very different from those who have been dispossessed in the execution of the schemes. Have the Council felt themselves unable to cope with the inevitable difficulties of management?

These various considerations lead to the inference that, however much in earnest the councillors of London may be at present in taking up the work of house-building, they are not likely in the result to effect improvement in the quality of the homes of wage-earners.

Nor are they likely to prove more successful in adding to the quantity of them. The entrance of the State as a competitor in the business is in many ways a danger to those who provide houses in order to earn a profit. The State has immense resources and wields coercive power. Opinion is in an unsettled condition as to the proper use and limits of this power. Those who are seeking employment for their capital can show good reason for preferring forms of investment which do not lie under the menace of public bodies.

House-building in London, moreover, will be unfavourably affected in specific ways if the State undertake large building operations. The cost of building is likely to be enhanced or kept at a high rate. The London County Council has appeared in the field as a master builder, who provides work on terms which suit those who prefer a high reward of labour to a low cost of building. The Council submits thereby to the irony of fate. It undertakes the work in order to benefit those who need houses. It so conducts it as to confer a privilege on those who build houses, to the detriment of those who need them. When, moreover, the houses are once built, at whatever cost, the State cannot avert such a fall in rents as may be brought about by economic causes, such as new facilities of transport or a change in trade conditions. However sincerely those who manage on the State's behalf may intend to make the houses self-supporting, the result depends on causes beyond their control—viz., the relation between demand and supply. The good intentions of the managers will not enable them to get more rent than the tenants will pay. It will seem proper to make the houses fulfil the purpose of their construction as homes for wage-earners, and to keep them fully occupied even at a still greater reduction in rentals. The effect of such a competition on the respective owners will be different. As regards the buildings owned by the councils, the guarantee of the ratepayers is always at hand to supply any deficiency. To private owners, on the other hand, the competition may bring such a reduction of profit as will check the growth of the business and impair its efficiency. It is not only, be it observed, the actual incidence of these drawbacks, but the fear of them which deters investors. The enterprise or ingenuity of business men presents a wide choice to those who have capital to employ. Forms of investment compete against each other for the favour of investors. A drawback, therefore, to a particular form of investment, if it turn the scale in favour of other forms, may have a deterrent effect wholly disproportionate to its intrinsic gravity. Thus the backward condition of all matters depending on electricity in this country is attributed by many persons to the grasping disposition displayed by the State as regards the options of purchase conferred upon municipal bodies.

Voluntary enterprise, as has been shown, is conducting the business of house-building in London and the neighbourhood on a gigantic scale. Any drawback, therefore, which touches the business as an investment, and diminishes the flow of capital into it, will affect very large sums of money and prevent the building of very many houses.

The competition of the State is clearly such a drawback; it is formidable, and looms still more formidable in the eyes of prudent or timid investors.

It may, indeed, fairly be inferred that the more houses the State builds, the more houses will it prevent other people from building. The building work of the councils, however actively carried on, is likely to cause a loss and not a gain in the number of houses erected for wage-earners. Both in quantity and in quality the State is likely to prove a less efficient instrument than voluntary enterprise for the improvement of the homes of the people.

CHAPTER VI.

PUBLIC DANGERS OF MUNICIPAL BUILDING.

A STAGNATING effect on the business of providing houses is only one of many drawbacks incidental to the new proposals.

The county councils and the borough councils have important functions and duties to perform with respect to the supervision of buildings; they are charged to see that the provisions of the Public Health Acts and the Building Acts are fulfilled. They have, moreover, been entrusted in some cases with a discretion to mitigate the severity of the regulations; they have been made umpires between the State and the owner, between the public welfare and the interest of the particular enterprise. The determination of these matters, in whatever form presented, is a judicial act of a responsible character.

A popularly elected body may not be a

very suitable authority for the discharge of judicial duties. Such a body is inclined to approach the matter in the spirit of an administrator rather than of a judge, and to act as if the land within its jurisdiction were its own estate.

Now these councils are the authorities empowered to act on behalf of the State in providing houses for wage-earners. There is an awkwardness in the double position of supervisors and owners. It seems impolitic that those who are charged with the duty of supervising buildings should plunge into the building trade as competitors with the very owners whom it is their duty to supervise. Investors already alarmed at the prospect of State competition and by the stringency of State supervision, will not be reassured by an arrangement which commits the supervision of their buildings to a rival builder.

There is a further point. Governments, even though democratic, are instruments for the attainment of certain ends. It is idle to expect from them results which they are not fitted to secure. As instruments for the provision of houses for wage-earners,

councils elected under a democratic franchise
labour under special disadvantages. The
members are subject to a perpetual inducement to show results in order to attract
votes. They are under pressure to build
something somewhere. The belief in the
efficacy of intervention by Government is
widespread. The advocates of a definite
plan of public action, whatever be its intrinsic
value, have the advantage of inviting electors
to walk by sight and not by faith. The play
of social and economic forces may be a more
effective instrument than State intervention
for the provision of house-room, but electors
who complain of high rentals are hard to
convince of it. The buildings to be erected
by the State loom largely in prospect; they
promise to be themselves moderate in rental,
and to effect by their competition a reduction
in the general scale of rentals. The house-
building under voluntary auspices, which
the competition of the State will check or
prevent, is necessarily out of sight and
probably out of mind.

Unfortunately, this is not the worst which
happens. It is impossible to avoid the

conclusion that the demand on the State for
the provision of houses is made as much in
the interests of the wage-earners who build the
houses, as of those who are to live in them.
The London County Council has not deemed
it sufficient to provide houses; they have
themselves become builders and employers
of labour on a large scale. They have in all
respects shown themselves subservient to
the trades unions. A Works Department
has been created which disburses immense
sums of public money in wages and materials,
with the result that large resources become
available for the purposes of the trades
unions. The excellence of the County
Council as a model employer of labour is
testified in the costliness of its buildings.

The members of the Council on their side
acquire the dignity, the patronage, and the
other advantages which the management of
a great department confers.

Considering the number of persons influ-
enced by these various considerations, it is not
wonderful that the intervention of the State
finds numerous and enthusiastic advocates.

In thinking of the relations between the

London County Council and Labour, the mind is led on to reflect on the immense possibilities of evil which attend the adoption of great building schemes by the councils in London. The record of the Works Department of the County Council presages that when the broom has grown older it may become even less clean in its sweeping. Building operations involve complicated transactions. Sites must be purchased, legal rights determined, compensation made, contracts concluded, materials purchased. An army of people has to be employed in various capacities. What infinite possibilities are opened out, not only of extravagance, but also of wire-pulling, jobbery, and the feathering of nests in multitudinous ways. There is abundant evidence that under similar inducements and with similar opportunities these evils have arisen and tend to arise. No sufficient justification has been shown for running such risks, for exposing the virtue of many to such temptation, for imposing on the public generally the burden of being ever watchful and alert lest these evils should arise.

But the difficulties are not yet exhausted. A municipality which has built dwellings on a large scale will be the landlord of a correspondingly large number of tenants. Is not this a position fraught with danger ? If the municipal dwellings are let at current rates of rental, an agitation is likely to arise to compel the municipality to show itself a model landlord as well as a model employer of labour, and to let houses cheaply which it has built dearly. Such arguments may appeal to those of the voters who are or who hope to be tenants of the municipality. Should a profit be earned—an unlikely contingency—the last-mentioned agitation may be met by a claim to apply the profits in relief of the existing ratepayers. Already the financial policy of the London County Council has been criticised on the ground that it will result through the operation of the sinking fund in the acquisition by the ratepayers of a valuable property at the expense of the tenants of the municipality. If, on the other hand, the municipal dwellings are let at rentals below the current rate, those who have not the good fortune to be tenants of the municipality will have a grievance. The municipal ownership of dwellings, indeed, seems likely to promote rather than to allay agitation and discontent, and to display municipal institutions as instruments of personal advantage rather than of the public good.

This drawback, unfelt at first, will become more and more serious as the municipal estate increases. The prospect is alarming to those who care about the tone and the standard of public life in our municipalities.

The municipal buildings, moreover, will exert influences of a more subtle kind. They will stand as object-lessons in dependence, teaching the workmen to look for the supply of desirable things to sources other than themselves and their own exertions. Why should they not proceed to press upon the State demands for still cheaper locomotion, for cheap food, or cheap fuel? The ideal which has inspired much of the great and successful striving of wage-earners after the welfare of their class has been that of complete economic independence at all stages and under all circumstances of life. Nothing less than this will bring abiding satisfaction. Not a little that happens in these days is calculated to obscure this ideal. Great, therefore, is the responsibility of those who, by public proposals or private action, place temptation in the way of the weaker brethren and smooth the descent to dependence. The matter, too, has a practical side. Any branch of human activity which is withdrawn from the free play of competition is in danger of suffering decay. Mind ceases to exert itself in that branch; improvement slackens and then ceases; action becomes mechanical. Society thus suffers decay of function. It may even lose the power of adaptation. Some ants, we are told by naturalists, have enslaved other ants, and compelled their captives to feed them, with the result that they have lost the power of feeding themselves.

The several drawbacks which have been mentioned in this chapter as attending the intervention of the State in the matter of housing the people will appeal with different force to different minds. Taken together they present a strong case.

These perils and inconveniences, moreover, will be incurred without any certain prospect of improving the homes of the people. On the contrary, there is good reason to think, as has been shown in the last chapter, that the entrance of the State as a competitor in the business of building and owning houses is likely to have an unfavourable influence on the houses of wage-earners.

CHAPTER VII.

SANITARY DEFECTS AND MUNICIPAL BUILDING.

THE insanitary conditions under which some wage-earners live are among the most effective pleas in support of the demand that the State should undertake the work of house-building. Unhealthy areas, plague spots, slums, close courts, tumble-down houses, underground cellars, overcrowded rooms, play a prominent part in popular discussion. People do not pause to think whether the advent of the State, as builder and landlord, is the appropriate remedy, or any remedy at all, for these evils. The wand of the councils will, it is assumed, effect a transformation. It seems well, therefore, to examine these insanitary conditions in some detail. They fall conveniently into groups.

Houses may be unfitted in design and structure to accommodate the number of families which inhabit them. This is a very common defect. Large areas of London are composed of cottages designed as the home of one family, but now occupied by several families living under defective sanitary conditions.

Houses, too, may be ill-designed, with insufficient space, light, and air, like some new block dwellings and many old courts and alleys.

Houses, again, may be badly built, or may be allowed to fall into disrepair.

In all such cases, which form the first group, the unhealthy conditions flow from defective structure.

Defects in structure suggest improvement in structure. This idea has lain at the root of the efforts which have been hitherto made to improve the housing of wage-earners in London. The keynote of these efforts has been the substitution of healthy houses for houses very much the reverse. A large measure of success has been attained by the co-operation of many forces.

The administration of the sanitary laws, the pressure of public opinion, the growing consciousness of the responsibilities of ownership, the efforts of philanthropists, and other forces have led to considerable amelioration of the sanitary condition of houses ; but the main instrument of improvement has been the voluntary activity of those who, as large or small investors, have provided dwellings in the hope of receiving a satisfactory return upon the capital expended. It may be that the demand has not been met adequately, but insufficiency is no new or exceptional thing in human affairs, and is likely to survive the intervention of the councils. Reasons, indeed, have been given in previous chapters for the conclusion that the councils are likely to prove less effective instruments of improvement in houses than the voluntary activity which they will displace.

The second group is of a wholly different character, and presents greater difficulties. Insanitary conditions may exist in houses which comply with all reasonable requirements as regards design, structure, or state of repair. These evils, indeed, are sometimes found in houses which are new and

apparently well built. The unhealthy conditions arise ˏfrom the careless, dirty, and
degraded habits of the occupants.

The mischief is not confined to those who
are poor in the sense that their earning
powers are small.   Self-contained tenements
commanding a substantial rent are sometimes found to be in a most filthy condition.
There is, moreover, in the keeping of tenements every degree in the downward scale.
Some persons, indeed, though neither criminal
nor immoral, have acquired or reverted
to destructive habits; they seem to have lost
all feeling for the home as the spot where
the duties and graces of family life, where
comfort, decency, and order receive a local
habitation and a name.   It has been publicly
suggested that such uncivilised people
should be housed in tiled rooms, into which
a hose could be turned every morning.   The
provision of loose boxes, however, will not
satisfy those who regard the home as a root
of excellence in the individual and in the
community, and who have faith in the ideals
of which it is the outward and visible sign.
Far other is the aspiration of workers who

strive by the persuasion of their personal influence to re-establish the home as the seat of family life. The fruit of such work may ripen slowly, and apart from the public gaze, but it ripens surely, and bears within it the promise of the future.

Still deeper in the mire have sunk those who have given up the attempt to maintain a home of their own. A striking example is found in the tenements let as " furnished rooms " in some parts of London. A few " sticks " of furniture are put into the room, and it is let at 1s. a night, or 6s. to 7s. a week, to anyone who will pay the rent in advance ; no questions are asked as to the relationship of the occupants to each other, nor is demur made to their number. Such houses are in effect lodging-houses for the promiscuous use of men, women, and children, and are, as the law stands at present, free from inspection under the Common Lodging-Houses Acts. Experience shows that the occupants have for the most part lost their homes, and come down to a " furnished room," through excess in drink or irregularity of domestic relationship. Moral degradation is the most striking and the most serious feature in such cases, but squalor and overcrowding are common. The sort of people who inhabit " furnished rooms " tend to aggregate together; like attracts like.   Particular streets, courts, and alleys thus become notorious, and a plague spot is formed which is great in mischief even if small in area.

In such cases the unhealthy conditions arise from the misconduct of those who control and of those who inhabit the houses.   The owners profit by the vices of the occupiers. No re-arrangement of bricks and mortar, no labour of the builder, the plumber, or the cleanser will heal the mischief.   An effort is being made in some places to bring "furnished rooms " within the Common Lodging-Houses Acts.   Inspection may be beneficial in the interests of decency, cleanliness, and order, but a thorough cure will only ensue from a change in the character and the habits of both owner and occupier which make these conditions of life possible.   Those who are conversant with the tenants of these " furnished rooms " will agree that sickness, misfortune, or poverty alone seldom bring anyone to prolonged residence in them. It is not a cheap way of living. The rent charged for one miserable "furnished room" approximates to the rent of two unfurnished rooms in a respectable house in the same neighbourhood. The attraction to such a life lies in freedom from moral restraint. Seemliness of living, indeed, depends on character rather than on means, as is shown by the very large number of quite poor people who have creditable homes.

Akin in effect to the "furnished rooms" are the shelters which have been established in some parts of London, where accommodation is offered gratuitously or for a very small payment. The unfortunate people who nightly resort to the shelters are herded promiscuously together, without enquiry or discrimination, in a way that promotes the spread of disease and tends to the corruption of the less depraved. The shelters, moreover, invite men to neglect their families and encourage irresponsible habits of life.

In the second group, therefore, the defect lies in the character and conduct of those who hire, and sometimes of those who let, the tenements ; insanitary conditions follow upon a degraded way of life. It will be noted that the quality of the home is determined by the habits of the occupiers. Dwellings, therefore, ought not to be treated as if they are things apart from the character and habits of the actual or prospective tenants. It is idle to expect rough people to become smooth on change of dwelling place. Those, therefore, who are minded to provide houses for wage-earners will do well to retain control of them, or at least to place them in responsible hands, lest the last state of them be worse than the first.

It seems clear that from no point of view does the advent of the State as a builder and owner of houses appear to be remedial of the evils which flow from the moral defects of owners and occupiers. The root of the mischief is not want of means or want of houses, but want of character. In the more flagrant instances the State, as the guardian of the public health, may have a more suitable ground of interference. These instances of overcrowding and squalor point to the need of the enforcement of existing sanitary laws. There is less hardship in the enforcement of these laws than is often assumed. The obligation to find more healthy accommodation draws out latent forces. It may lead to a diminution of expenditure on things which profit not, or to the use of increased effort to find more or better paid work, or to the better management of income, or to the conquest of mere inertness and dislike of change.

It is desired to lay special stress on these various considerations. It seems clear that confusion of mind is prevalent between the function of the State as guardian of the public health and as a purveyor of commodities such as houses. Though the State be active in house-building, the need for the enforcement of sanitary laws will remain until the defects of character be amended which give rise to the breaches of the law. It is sometimes said that there is a difficulty in enforcing sanitary laws, because sufficient accommodation does not exist to house the overcrowded. This statement does not seem to be borne out by facts, except, perhaps, in

very limited areas.   At a reasonable distance
rooms can be found by those who are willing
to pay the current rentals.   However this
may be, it seems unlikely that in districts
which attract more than a full complement
of residents, the erection of buildings either
by the State or by voluntary enterprise
will meet this particular difficulty ; the new
buildings will soon be filled and the margin
of accommodation left for the dispossessed
will be as small as before.

The existence of insanitary conditions,
therefore, relevant enough for the consideration of the State as the administrator of the
sanitary laws, is beside the mark when urged
as a reason for pressing the State to become
a builder and owner of houses.

The third group of insanitary conditions
arises from overcrowding pure and simple.
The tenements may be suitable in design and
structure to be the homes of a reasonable
number of occupants, and the residents may
be of average respectability, but the number
of the occupants is excessive having regard
to the size of the rooms.   Such overcrowding is mainly caused by the pressure of a

population in which the sanitary sense is still insufficiently developed.

The remedy which springs into the mind for a deficiency in house-room is the provision of more house-room. It appears, accordingly, that in recent discussions the cry has been for new buildings. It is in quantity rather than in quality that houses are now thought to be deficient. Far from demurring to this demand, it is a chief aim of this volume to indicate the methods and conditions likely to bring the most new buildings into existence. There seems, however, little hazard in forecasting that municipal efforts in house-building will fail to take away the reproach of insufficiency. New dwellings built in the suburbs will only add to the immense number of houses already built in them, and will compete with those in which overcrowding is not alleged rather than with the dwellings in more central and crowded districts. Moreover, the cost price of all new houses in the suburbs, no less than in the centre, is at present high, and will not afford much opportunity of attracting occupants by cheap rentals. If, on the other

hand, the new houses are built in more central
districts, they will, if of good design and
construction, add to the attractive forces of
those districts, and allure people back from
the suburbs.

The causes of the present pressure of
population in London are clear. The
country has for some years been prosperous; work has been more regular and
better paid, and the wage-earner has
enjoyed ampler means. Increased prosperity has been accompanied by a rise in
the standard of living, which includes a
demand for more house-room. The Census,
as has been shown, gives evidence of a
spreading-out of the population. In some
districts there has been an influx of foreigners,
who annex street after street by buying out
the previous residents. A decrease has con-
currently occurred in the space available for
dwelling houses in the more central districts.
The same prosperity which has given wage-
earners a larger command of money has
caused a larger proportion of the space to
be devoted to railways, streets, docks, warehouses, offices and other purposes of business

and locomotion. Moreover, increased and ever-increasing demands on the space available for building are being made in the interests of light and air, and other things needful to the public health.

This condition of things encourages wage-earners to practise economy in house-room —an excessive economy, as it appears to their critics. The diffusion of the population which is in progress leads to the hope that the benefits of space and air are being more esteemed by wage-earners. Increased attention, however, to the conditions of healthy living is certainly to be desired.

An owner may select a salubrious site, may secure to every room an abundant current of air, and may provide ample means of ventilation ; but it lies with the occupant to enjoy or to reject the full benefit. He may, if he will, seal up many of the inlets so carefully provided. It is found, indeed, that occupants frequently show ingenuity and industry in defending their homes from invasion by alien air. The virtues of fresh air are not yet fully appreciated by many wage-earners; travellers may be seen filling up a compartment in a railway train to its full complement, without a glance to see whether the next compartment be less crowded. Houses of wage-earners are often found to be airless and stuffy, quite apart from any indication of overcrowding, or poverty, or want of cleanliness. The sanitary sense of many seems to be still imperfectly developed. This defective sense of the value of fresh air is due to many causes—ignorance of the conditions of health; long established use and habit; economy in fuel and in the labour of cleaning; for with London air comes in London dirt.

The defective appreciation of the value of air prevalent among wage-earners is very relevant to the question of overcrowding. The home is contracted within narrower bounds, or a lodger is introduced in order to ease the pressure of rent. The amount so saved in rent may procure better food or clothing, or may represent other uses and enjoyments which are both pressing and reasonable. The occupier's choice between these competing advantages largely depends upon the value which he attaches to fresh air.

The mischief, it may be noted, extends

beyond the tenement affected at the moment; the overcrowding enables the occupier to pay a higher rent, and tends to keep up the general level of rentals, with the result that others are tempted to overcrowd their tenements in like manner.

It may be added that a recognition of the conditions of healthy living in all classes of the community is of recent origin and imperfect.

A wage-earner living in a central district, pressed by a rising rent or a growing family, may indeed remove his home to the suburbs, and accept the additional burden of going to and fro. This alternative is largely adopted by people in all classes, but residence in central districts has strong and obvious attractions, and the vacant places are soon filled.

Wage-earners have the further choice of increasing their income by extra exertion, or of reducing their expenditure by retrenchment. These expedients may in particular cases be neither feasible nor desirable. Many people are already working to the extent of or beyond their powers, and find that an increase in rent entails deprivation in food, clothing, or warmth.

It is clear, nevertheless, that among large sections of the people there is ample scope for increase of productiveness or for decrease of expenditure. There is a large amount of unskilled labour of both men and women, which might by better education and training be made more valuable. A mine of national wealth remains in this respect unworked; many persons, too, who possess skill, do not use it to advantage, through lack of industry or of stability of character; immense sums, moreover, are spent on alcoholic drink and other forms of unprofitable expenditure in which retrenchment is in every way desirable. In the arts of household management, too, there is much room for improvement. The acquisition of a taste for fresh air would be doubly blest if it led people to develop their skill or to check waste. Civilisation largely consists in the victory of gainful over wasteful desires.

It may be thought that if the bulk of wage-earners become possessed of a desire for more space and more air in their homes, the effect will be to increase the demand for house-room, and to raise still higher the level of rent. Undoubtedly, if crowding is to be less, accommodation must be more. Additional house-room, however, is being provided on an immense scale in less central districts. The refusal of wage-earners to live under very crowded conditions involves migration to districts where improved accommodation is to be found. There seems no reason to doubt that commercial enterprise is equal to the task of coping with this demand. The causes which affect the level of rents are complex and difficult. It seems clear, how-ever, that overcrowding produces high rents as truly as high rents produce overcrowding. There is action and reaction. A rise, there-fore, in the standard of wage-earners' requirements as regards space and air is likely to lessen overcrowding without raising rentals.

So far, then, as overcrowding is caused by a deficiency in the sanitary sense of large sections of wage-earners, the advent of the State as a purveyor of houses is not likely to prove remedial of the evil. The houses built by the State will doubtless be filled, but the crowding elsewhere will remain as thick as before. It seems, then, that the existence of the sanitary evils referred to in this chapter due to defects in structure, or to a low standard of conduct, or to mere overcrowding, afford no sufficient ground for the proposed intervention of the State as a builder and owner of houses.

CHAPTER VIII.

SANITARY DEFECTS AND AN IMPROVED ART OF LIVING.

A DETAILED discussion of the remedies for the ·sanitary evils referred to in the last chapter lies beyond the scope of this volume. It may not, however, be out of place to make some observations upon the forces which are working towards a better state of things.

The improvement which has taken place of late years in the housing of wage-earners forms part of a rise in the standard of living. It is natural, therefore, to infer that further improvement in housing will depend upon the progress and extension of this general amelioration.   The inference is especially strong in respect of the insanitary conditions which are produced by ignorance and carelessness.

A rise in the standard of living depends on the coincidence of a variety of forces. The mere arrangement or re-arrangement of

bricks and mortar is the simplest part of the
affair. It is only proposed to indicate certain
salient features. In order to make existing
resources yield an increased benefit, there
is need of efforts which are both intellectual
and moral. An increased knowledge of the
properties of things will bring a truer ap-
praisement of their value and altered views
as to their use; while the application of the
new knowledge to the circumstances of life
will oftentimes demand a change in conduct,
and will lead to a change in the objects of
desire. Who, for example, can estimate the
advance in morals and civilisation which will
follow upon an increase of knowledge of the
true value of alcoholic drink as an article of
diet, and a corresponding decrease in the
desire for it? The application of knowledge
to the circumstances of life constitutes the
art of living. Experience is the great teacher
of the art; but the experience which per-
suades need not be the personal experience
of the man persuaded. Experience becomes
crystallised in law, custom, and literature;
it moulds the ruling ideals; it works through
the imitative instincts, through susceptibility

to opinion, and by the personal persuasions of those who influence the people by religious, charitable, and social work. It is part of the irony of things that not a little of the work of the last-mentioned group consists in shielding people from the consequences of their acts, and thereby weakening the instructive force of experience.

Improvement in the art of living, as it advances under the influence of experience, is the principal force which is proving, and will continue to prove, remedial of a large part of the sanitary evils described in the last chapter. The benefits of cleanliness and fresh air are being more widely appreciated. The conditions of health are becoming better understood. The education of the sanitary sense is making progress.

It is well, however, to be cautious in anticipation, and to remember that the rate at which improvement makes itself felt is necessarily slow. Time is required for an increase of knowledge and for a change in habits and objects of desire. The poorer folk have ever lagged behind the rest of the community in matters of hygiene.

It must, moreover, be clearly recognised that a section of those who live in unhealthy surroundings are little amenable to reasonable considerations. The victims of vices, such as drunkenness and gambling, oftentimes adhere to their ruinous ways in spite of their personal experience of the miseries which their misconduct produces. The vicious habits of such will yield only to those religious and moral influences which change the character.

There is another point to be noticed concerning advancement in the art of living. Improvement in this art implies that people not only know more and are willing to change old habits and old desires at the bidding of new knowledge, but also have the material means of effecting these changes. An improved standard of living may involve an increased cost of living. This consideration may in some conditions of society be of paramount importance. It is at present of moment to some of the poorest whose struggle to live is intensified by ever-increasing public burdens. It is certain, however, that the bulk of wage-earners have it in their power to meet reasonable changes in their way of living from the economies resulting from those very changes. The most marked, though by no means the only instance, is found in the enormous expenditure of wage-earners on alcoholic drink, to which reference has been made.

The way of improvement through an increase of knowledge and of self-control, though slow—too slow for a hasty age—is sure, because it implies improvement in the character of the people themselves. It is not imposed on them from without ; it grows out of their own sense of fitness, as a flower from a root ; it contains within itself the promise of continuance and stability. Faith in such a method of growth is inconsistent with confidence in any such short cut to improvement as the imposition of responsibility for the supply of houses upon municipal bodies. Reasons have been given for thinking that this device will not prove a remedy for the sanitary evils complained of, and will not result in procuring for wage-earners better houses and more of them. The proposal may lull uneasy feelings that something should be done, but it diverts the minds of men from the healthy way of improvement, and uses up wastefully energies which might be employed in directing the thoughts and actions of men into more profitable channels.

CHAPTER IX.

GROWTH OF PUBLIC BURDENS.

THE growth of public burdens, especially in the form of municipal rates, has a marked bearing on the prospects of free commercial enterprise as applied to house-building. The matter is also worthy of consideration by those advocates of municipal house-building who desire that the buildings should continue to be self-supporting. There seems in these days to be no limit to the demands on the public purse, except the exhaustion in means or in patience of those who have to pay the bill. There is no difficulty in advancing cogent reasons for increased expenditure on any subject which awakens special interest. Claims of ever-increasing costliness are thus made in relation to the army and navy, to the relief of the distressed and the maintenance of the aged, to the education of the young, to science and art, to improved sanitation and open spaces, and to many other things. It may be conceded that excellence in these matters is desirable ; it does not, however, follow that it is desirable to take the means of promoting it by force from the pockets of the people. A high standard of excellence and of costliness may be suitable to those who are well-to-do, but the poorer part of the population need arrangements which are simpler and less expensive. No system of compulsory taxation has been devised which will prevent costliness, which is suitable to some, from pressing with undue severity upon others. This difficulty is well illustrated in connection with the business of house-building.

Moneys are collected by the rates for a varied assortment of purposes. These include certain branches of the civil administration which undertake the protection of person and property, the enforcement of sanitary laws, and the maintenance of streets and roads. These purposes may have an immediate bearing on the utility, and therefore on the value of the property rated.

There are, however, included in the rates a variety of imposts which have a very remote bearing on the value of the property rated. Typical instances are found in the relief of the poor and the education of the young. The duties of assisting destitute neighbours and of educating other men's children may or may not form part of the general obligations of good citizenship; these duties, however, have no special reference to the occupancy of houses. It is the social order as a whole which is menaced by destitution or ignorance, and not the particular kind of property which consists in houses. The cost of these different purposes is met by a rate levied on land and houses according to the market value of the right to occupy and use them in their existing condition. Thus, the rateable value of a shop, factory, or warehouse is fixed on the basis of assessing the rent which a tenant may be expected to give for it for trade purposes, having regard to its size, accommodation and position. A dwelling-house is rated on the basis of a similar enquiry into its value as a place of residence.

Dwelling-houses, moreover, seem ill-suited to be a basis of taxation. Space and air in the home are important to health and well-being ; it is mischievous, therefore, to tax people in proportion as their houses are spacious and airy. A man is not rated on his wealth—viz., his capacity to provide himself with all manner of commodities ; he is rated on his user of a particular commodity—viz., a dwelling-house. The size of his house is largely determined by the necessities of his family. The greater, therefore, the private claims upon him, the heavier is his public burden ; the more effectively he does his duty towards those for whom he is responsible, the more he has to pay for the benefit of those for whom he is not responsible.

This method of imposing public burdens has the incidental disadvantage that it is likely to prove detrimental to the growth of the business of house-building.

The incidence of taxation is a delicate matter to handle. Some points, however, are clear, and suffice for the present purpose. The occupier's liability in respect of his house-room includes rates as well as rent. It is, indeed, a common practice in London that the landlord should make an inclusive charge for rent, rates and water rate. The tenant can only occupy a particular tenement if the total sum which represents his liability be within his means. An excess in either rent or rates which brings his total liability beyond the sum which he is willing to spend in house-room will provoke him to seek cheaper accommodation. This possible result of increased rating is becoming important. The profit which the erection of dwellings for wage-earners will yield, having regard to the cost price of site and building and to the rentals obtainable, tends to become only just sufficient to prove tempting to the owners of capital. In such a position an increase in the rates will make it difficult to erect new buildings, and prove detrimental to the growth of the business.

Some figures taken from the accounts of the East End Dwellings Company will show that rates are imposing a growing burden on house property.

Figures in respect to this company's dwellings erected previously to 1890 :—

Year.	Amount received from tenants. £	Percentage of such amount paid by the company for rates.
1890 ...	4,766 ...	12 per cent.
1895 ...	5,273 ...	15 „ „
1900 ...	5,560 ...	14½ „ „
1901 ...	5,599 ...	17 „ „

In the last year, therefore, rates absorbed nearly 3s. 5d. in the £1 of the total sums received, or about 1s. in 6s.

Similar figures in respect to the whole of the company's buildings :—

Year.	Amount received from tenants. £	Percentage of such amount paid by the company for rates.
1890 ...	4,766 ...	12 per cent.
1895 ...	15,802 ...	15½ „ „
1900 ...	24,419 ...	15 „ „
1901 ...	27,313 ...	16½ „ „

The housing business, moreover, seems to be prejudiced more than other businesses by a rise in rates. The shopkeeper, manufacturer, or warehouseman pays rates only on the rateable value of the premises on which the business is conducted, without regard to the turnover or the profits. Those who are interested in houses pay rates based on the whole return. A rising rate, therefore, tends to give an advantage to other businesses which compete with house purveying for the favour of investors.

These various considerations convey a significant warning. The objects for which rates are levied may be excellent, but the benefit will be all too dearly purchased at the expense of space and air in the homes of wage-earners.

CHAPTER X.

CONCLUSION.

DEFINITE drawbacks attend the advent of the State as a purveyor of houses on a large scale. The position of the councils as traders is inconsistent with their duties as administrators of the sanitary laws and supervisors of houses. Popularly elected bodies, moreover, are involved in difficulties and dangers when they carry on a large business and become employers of labour and landlords. The purity of public life and the manly independence of the individual are alike subjected to temptation. The councils, too, are unlikely to display the adaptability and other businesslike qualities which are needed to secure improvement in dwellings to meet ever-changing wants. It is plain, furthermore, that the assumption of responsibility by the State for the provision of houses will discourage voluntary enterprise.

What, then, are the reasons which are deemed to outweigh these grave considerations?

The most popular line of argument consists in denouncing sanitary defects. These evils, however, which are real enough, demand quite other remedies than the proposed intervention of the councils. As regards structural defects, immense progress has been made by the repair of insanitary houses and the substitution of new dwellings for old. The squalor, too, which sometimes accompanies moral degradation, calls for the application of existing sanitary laws rather than for the erection of new buildings by a public authority. A widespread deficiency, moreover, in the sanitary sense is responsible for much overcrowding, by which the burden of rent is eased at the expense of space and of air; overcrowding and high rents act and react on each other. Defects which arise from ignorance or carelessness will yield only to an increase of knowledge and a consequent improvement in the arts of living.

It seems clear from these various considerations that the existence of sanitary defects is no sufficient justification for the advent of the councils as purveyors of houses.

Another line of argument maintains that the action of the councils is necessary in order to get houses built at all. This argument ignores the great work done by voluntary enterprise in providing additional accommodation in Greater London during the decade 1891—1901 for more than a million persons. Even this statement does not represent the extent of the achievement. Voluntary enterprise during the decade, besides adding to the London of 1891 the equivalent of a huge city, has built improved dwellings to a great

houses standing in 1891. Thus in a great area of Central London, containing more than a million of inhabitants, the population has been practically stationary since 1891, with the result that every new house built in the area during the decade is in substitution for a house or houses standing at that date.

These facts demonstrate the vitality of the business of house-building and dispose of the contention that houses will not be built unless the State intervene to build them.

In a matter of such magnitude it is proper to take a broad view. A great movement of population is taking place. An increase of accommodation is being provided which is needed owing to three distinct causes: (1) the excess, past and present, of births over deaths; (2) the attractive power of the metropolitan area; (3) the transfer of population within the area of Greater London due to commercial development. The figures are colossal; it is not the failure but the success of commercial enterprise in dealing with so great a movement which is surprising.

Movements of this kind inevitably produce hardship. The value of land for commercial as distinguished from residential purposes tends to rise in the centres of industry. The area of increased values expands outwards. As each street is successively affected the rise in value brings change and possibly hardship to those whose homes, like the sand castles of the children, are overwhelmed by the flowing tide. From these strokes of fortune none can claim exemption; the changes and chances of life touch each and all in turn, and affect now one commodity and now another. They are the outcome of industrial development; they form no sufficient ground for the proposed intervention of the State.

It appears, furthermore, that the assumption of responsibility by the State for the provision of houses will not benefit wage-earners. The efforts of the State and of voluntary enterprise cannot flourish together; reasoning and experience unite in showing their incompatibility. The more the State builds the less will voluntary enterprise accomplish. Alike in quantity and in quality, the displacement of commercial activity by public effort in house-building is likely to cause a loss to wage-earners.

It is to be remembered that many of the drawbacks which attend the action of the councils are not matters of speculation; they have arisen and are sure to grow; whereas the advantage to be gained by the action of the councils is conjectural and depends on the degree to which voluntary enterprise is deterred by its public rival. Certain damage is, therefore, being incurred for an uncertain prospect of benefit.

The demand for State intervention is based on an inadequate recognition of the facts, and a lack of faith in the principles which form the mainspring of beneficial activity in a free industrial community.

In such a community the demand of those who desire commodities, and are able and willing to pay for them, determines the application of labour and capital to their production. Demand moulds supply with ever-increasing precision, and has developed in those who carry on the work the moral and mental qualities which promote efficiency. It is the market which demonstrates the things which the people really care about; it tests desires. The market, therefore, is the surest guide to policy, in so far, at any rate, as it may be proper to promote the fulfilment of desires. The market, moreover, fixes the price of commodities with a propriety otherwise unattainable. It is the surest guide to price.

On all grounds, therefore, the free play of commercial forces has shown itself to be the most effective and suitable instrument of supply.

The interference of the State in the supply of houses has, upon examination, been found to be quite unlikely to procure for wage-earners better houses and more of them. Municipal action, moreover, is fraught with difficulties and dangers sufficient to deter from the enterprise those who desire to shield the paths of public life from obvious temptations.

CENSUS OF ENGLAND AND WALES, 1901.

County of London.

TABLE XIX.—*Total Tenements, and Tenements of less than Five Rooms, distinguishing those occupied by various numbers of Persons, in the County of London, 1891¹ and 1901.*

Rooms in Tenement.	Tenements of less than Five Rooms, 1891 and 1901.	Persons per Tenement.											
		1.	2.	3.	4.	5.	6.	7.	8.	9.	10.	11.	12 or more.
Total Tenements— 1891—937,606 1901—1,019,546		60,114 60,421	55,766 48,341	29,005 23,680	16,111 11,279	7,409 4,001	2,871 1,257	879 384	231 103	72 39	27 10	10 3	7 6
1 {	1891—172,502 1901—149,524	60,114 60,421	55,766 48,341	29,005 23,680	16,111 11,279	7,409 4,001	2,871 1,257	879 384	231 103	72 39	27 10	10 3	7 6
2 {	1891—189,707 1901—201,431	16,106 16,148	46,075 52,369	40,168 46,782	32,486 35,828	24,013 23,885	15,526 14,508	8,863 7,283	4,195 3,055	1,590 1,118	488 328	138 101	59 26
No. of Tenements of less than five rooms— 1891—630,569 1901—672,030		5,522 6,288	27,246 35,070	29,151 39,252	26,796 32,954	22,657 25,392	17,293 18,607	11,953 12,026	7,078 6,820	3,446 3,269	1,377 1,251	470 410	200 203
3 {	1891—153,189 1901—181,542	5,522 6,288	27,246 35,070	29,151 39,252	26,796 32,954	22,657 25,392	17,293 18,607	11,953 12,026	7,078 6,820	3,446 3,269	1,377 1,251	470 410	200 203
4 {	1891—115,171 1901—139,533	1,864 2,252	12,049 15,360	16,645 22,905	18,896 24,839	18,175 22,824	16,294 18,424	12,801 13,871	8,952 9,330	5,203 5,371	2,573 2,733	1,150 1,110	569 514

1 The figures for 1891 refer to the County of London as then constituted. The slight changes which have since been made in the area (*see* Note to Table 3) do not seriously affect the value of the figures for purposes of comparison.

NOTE.—The Table is to be read as follows:—Of the 1,019,546 tenements, 672,030 were tenements of less than five rooms, and of these 149,524 were tenements of one room, 201,431 of two rooms etc. and of the 149,524 tenements of one room, 60,421 were occupied by one person each, 48,341 by two persons each, etc.

INDEX.

AIR and space, value of, insufficiently appreciated, 89, 92

BUILDING, cost of:
Increase in, 54
State operations affecting, 64

CENSUS, 1901, housing statistics, 11, 15, 115
Cressy House, Stepney Green, description of, 41
Cromer Street Estate, King's Cross, description of, 41

DIRECTORS of housing companies, duties of, 44

EAST End Dwellings Company, 7, 19
Commercial success of, 50
History and work of, 36
Rates on houses of, 105
Efficiency of buildings, conditions of, 21
Occupiers' point of view, 24
Owners' point of view, 30

" FURNISHED rooms," evils of, 81

HEALTH statistics, East End Dwellings Company's buildings, 48

Hill, Miss Octavia, 37

INSANITARY conditions, causes of:
Habits of occupiers, 79
Lack of sanitary sense, 89
Structural defects, 77

KATHARINE Buildings, Aldgate, description of, 38

LADY managers of working-class dwellings, 39, 46
Lolesworth buildings, Spitalfields, description of, 39
London County Council:
Cost of building enhanced by operations of, 64
Housing returns to March, 1902, 13

MANAGEMENT of dwellings:
General conditions of efficiency, 34
Good management, importance of, 46
Lady managers, 39, 46
Personal qualities required for, 46
Resident superintendents, 41, 46
Selection and control of managers, 45

Municipal authorities, Inconsistent position as builders and supervisors of buildings, 69, 108

Municipal house-building: .
Arguments in favour of, 6
Cost of building enhanced by, 64
Inefficiency of, 57
Public dangers of, 68, 71, 72, 73, 74
Public improvements, in consequence of, 2
Sanitary defects, municipal house-building no cure for, 77, 84, 93
Unfavourable as regards quality and quantity, 59, 64

Museum Building, Bethnal Green, description of, 40

Occupiers' position and requirements, 23
Overcrowding:
Decrease in, 15, 85, 115
Defective sanitary sense causing, 86
High rentals, overcrowding an effect of, 93
Owners' position and requirements, 30

Peabody Trust, 36, 49
Pollard Houses, Pentonville, description of, 41
Public burdens, growth of, 101

Rating, effects of, upon :
East End Dwellings Company's buildings, 106
Housing business generally, 101
Resident superintendents of dwellings, 41, 46

Sanitary Defects, see Insanitary Conditions.
Shelters, evils of, 83
Single-roomed tenements, census statistics, 16, 115
Sites, cost, &c., 50, 52
Standard of living, causes of rise in, 88, 95
State Housing, see Municipal
Structural defects, insanitary conditions caused by, 77
Structural requirements of buildings, 43

Taxation, effects on housing business, 101
Tenements, number of, census statistics, 15, 115
Tenement Dwellings Company, 37
Three-room and two-room tenements, census statistics, 16
Types of tenements, 43

Variety in accommodation, need of, 25
Voluntary enterprise in house-building, vitality of, 11, 19

BRADBURY, AGNEW, & CO. LD., PRINTERS, LONDON AND TONBRIDGE.

P. S. KING & SON,

ESTABLISHED IN PARLIAMENT STREET, 1819.

ORCHARD HOUSE,
2 & 4, GREAT SMITH ST.,
WESTMINSTER.

Publishers,
Parliamentary and General Booksellers,
Bookbinders and Printers.

❦ ❦ ❦

Monthly Catalogue of all recent Parliamentary Papers, Reports, Bills, &c., also of the Reports issued by the INDIA OFFICE and GOVERNMENT OF INDIA, the LONDON COUNTY COUNCIL, the SCHOOL BOARD FOR LONDON, and other PUBLIC BODIES, and of Books and Pamphlets on Questions of the Day—Political, Economical, and Social. Post free.

❦ ❦ ❦

Books (New and Old).   Reports.
Parliamentary Papers.   Blue Books.
Pamphlets.   Official Publications, &c.

❦ ❦ ❦

LONDON COUNTY COUNCIL.

The Reports of the London County Council, consisting of the Annual Accounts, Reports on Water Supply, Public Health and Sanitary Matters, Fire Brigade, Works Department, Technical Education, Rating and Taxation, Statistics, &c., are published by P. S. KING & SON. *Catalogue, post free.*

SCHOOL BOARD FOR LONDON.

P. S. KING & SON are the appointed Publishers to the School Board for London, to whom all application for Reports and Publications issued by that body should be made. *Catalogue, post free.*

RECENT PUBLICATIONS BY

P. S. KING & SON, Westminster.

A HISTORY OF FACTORY LEGISLA-
TION. By B. L. HUTCHINS and A. HARRISON,
B.A. (Lond.). With Preface by SIDNEY WEBB.
10s. 6d. net.

ELEMENTS OF STATISTICS. By A. L.
BOWLEY, M.A. 10s. 6d. net.

HISTORY OF THE ENGLISH POOR LAW.
3 Vols. 42s. net.

LONDON WATER SUPPLY. By
H. C. RICHARDS, K.C., M.P., W. H. C. PAYNE,
and J. P. H. SOPER. Second Edition. 6s. net.

MUNICIPAL FINANCE AND MUNICIPAL
ENTERPRISE. By Right Hon. Sir H. H.
FOWLER, G.C.S.I., M.P. 1s.

OUR TREATMENT OF THE POOR. By
Sir WILLIAM CHANCE, M.A., Bart. 2s. 6d.

PUBLIC HEALTH AND HOUSING. By
JOHN F. J. SYKES, M.D., D.Sc. (Edin.). 5s. net.

SEWAGE WORKS ANALYSES. By GILBERT
J. FOWLER. 6s. net.

SOME FOOD DANGERS. By Sir JAMES
CRICHTON-BROWNE. 6d.

TAXATION, LOCAL AND IMPERIAL:
AND LOCAL GOVERNMENT. By J. C.
GRAHAM. Third Edition. 2s.

THE COST OF MUNICIPAL TRADING.
By DIXON H. DAVIES. 2s.

THE COTTAGE HOMES OF ENGLAND.
By W. WALTER CROTCH. Second Edition. 2s. net.

THE GOVERNMENT OF LONDON. By
J. RENWICK SEAGER. 2s. 6d.

THE PLACE OF COMPENSATION IN
TEMPERANCE REFORM. By C. P.
SANGER, M.A. 2s. 6d.

THE SANITARY INSPECTOR'S GUIDE.
By H. LEMMOIN-CANNON. 3s. 6d. net.

UNIVERSITY OF CALIFORNIA LIBRARY

THIS BOOK IS DUE ON THE LAST DATE
STAMPED BELOW

JUN 26 1916

OCT 31 1916

NOV 18 1916

APR 4 1919

DEC 1 1919

OC 1928

9Mr'65CS

30m-1,'15

Parsons.

157705

HD 7333
A5 P3

CPSIA information can be obtained
at www.ICGtesting.com
Printed in the USA
BVHW091344241218
536332BV00036B/2021/P